Let Your Faith Arise

Geary Reid

ISBN: 978-976-8305-55-8

Acknowledgments

Great thanks must be expressed to the following people:

The heavenly Father, for granting me the wisdom and inspiration to record the information in this book, which I began on August 25, 2021, and completed on August 28, 2021; my family, for their continued encouragement and support regarding various challenges; and several people who have assisted with reviewing and editing the book:

- Wonnette Nicholson, Dipl. in Business Management and Administration
- Roxanne Abrams-Ramprashad
- Rendell F. Harry

To you, the reader: have fun while reading, and grasp and practice what you learn so that this world will become a better place. Many people are depending on your guidance. We all need a shoulder to lean on and a hand to guide us.

Rev. Geary Reid
MBA, FCCA, FAAPM, MPM, CAT

Reid's Learning Institute and Business Consultancy

reidnlearn.com

Amazon: amazon.com/author/gearyreid

Facebook: Reid n Learn

Instagram: Reid n Learn

LinkedIn: Reid's Learning Institute
and Business Consultancy

199 Kuru - Kururu, Soesdyke Linden Highway
Guyana, South America

Table of Contents

Introduction

Many persons talk about faith, but not all of them actually walk in faith. Today is a great day to let your faith arise. When you take your faith to another level, you will experience the power and presence of God like never before. The world is looking at believers to see if they are walking in the faith they often talk about, so be a great example and practice living in faith.

In this refreshing literature, you will be provided with a clear definition of faith and supporting information to reinforce your understanding of faith. The definition is broken down into separate words, and each word is further explained with examples.

The word "faith" is supported by some important words that are often used by believers. Separate chapters are dedicated to those words which are synonymous with faith, and you will see how faith connects to these words.

If you are going to activate your faith, then you must know the word of God for yourself. Listening to the word of God helps to boost your faith. Those who live in faith will see many blessings following their lives, because it is God's intention to bless those who walk in faith.

Faith can change many things for those who believe in God. Hannah exercised her faith and God answered her prayer. King Hezekiah did not accept the first message from God that he would die soon, so he exercised his faith and prayed to God, and indeed God heard his prayer and increased his stay on the earth. Abraham had faith in God, and God counted his faith unto righteousness.

Without faith, no one can please God. Therefore, get faith now so that you can please God. No amount of riches can save anyone, but they must have faith in God and believe that Jesus is the only begotten Son of God who came to give them access to God's kingdom.

If you want to move from the pavilion to the podium, then walk in faith. Your name can be mentioned among many great believers if you walk in faith. When you walk in faith, those things that once seemed impossible to you will become possible. Even if your faith is like a mustard seed, it can still move mountains. Continue to build up your faith as you worship God and pray in the Holy Ghost.

Your faith will require you to wait on God. Allow God to work through you at his own time, but do not change your expectation of God. Your faith in God will contribute to your prosperity.

Continue to hope in God, as he will be there for you. Do not stop trusting God, as he will come through for you. Be confident that God will make great things happen for those who walk according to his will. Never cease to pray, as your breakthrough is soon to come. Have faith in God and not in man. Let your faith arise today in God and be a blessing to many persons.

1. Biblical words synonymous with faith

Figure 1 provides some essential words that persons need to know as they learn more about faith and exercise it. Faith is invisible to the human eye, but it becomes a reality in the form of trust, where believers place their confidence in God. If believers trust God so much, then they must pray to God, who has the ability to answer their prayers.

Figure 1. Essential ingredients for faith

(All figures developed by the author unless otherwise noted.)

No believer must lose hope in God's ability. Whatever he has said, he will perform it. However, believers must also exercise patience. They must wait for God to bring to pass the things they are trusting him to do.

Do not walk away empty-handed as a believer; know that God has many things for you. Let your faith arise and let people seek the evidence of your big and powerful God, who only wants to do good things for his people. Your understanding of faith will cause you to live in great expectation that many good this will happen for those are serving the Lord.

Table 1. Definitions of words synonymous with faith

Word	Explanations
Trust	Firm belief in the honesty, veracity, justice, strength, etc., of a person or thing. Place reliance in…
Wait	Abstain from action or departure till some expected event occurs; pause, tarry, stay.
Prayer	Solemn request to God or object of worship.
Confidence	Firm trust; assured expectation; boldness; impudence.
Hope	Expectation and desire combined.
Patience	Calm endurance of pain or any provocation; perseverance.

(Extracted from The Concise Oxford Dictionary of English, 5th edition, 1964)

2. What is faith, and is it necessary?

People often want great things to happen to them, so they keep wishing for such things. It is good for anyone to expect great things to happen to them. As a matter of fact, it is sad if persons are only anticipating that bad things will happen to them.

Sometimes, people have nothing to do with the things that happen to them. When some persons expect good things to happen to them, they are greeted by many bad things, and the opposite may be true for those who anticipate that bad things will happen to them and then realize that many good things have come their way.

2.1 What is faith?

There are many words and statements in the Bible for which persons have to use other literature and references to gather a true understanding. Sometimes, persons may have to use a dictionary for a concise interpretation of certain words. However, the word "faith" is used many times in the Bible, and the Bible also provides its definition. Therefore, believers do not have to look far to know what faith is. When persons have recently become saved and start using the Bible as part of their studies, they can immediately read about faith and know its definition, without having to get their church leaders to tell them what faith is.

Hebrews 11:1

1 Now faith is the substance of things hoped for, the evidence of things not seen.

For additional information to support your understanding of faith, Table 2 breaks Hebrews 11:1 down into smaller pieces, and many of the words are separately explained.

Table 2. Key words and their explanations from Hebrews 11:1

Word	Explanation
Now	Faith is always about the present and the future. It is never about the past. Therefore, faith cannot be retroactive: it cannot be used after an event has occurred. Faith is futuristic.
Is	The word "is" also speaks about the present and the future. Faith represents a singular thing, regardless of how big it is. Faith combines and compresses all situations into one. Faith does not consider what was, it considers what is, as faith is not looking back on the past.
Substance	Faith will have a substance, based upon each individual's request. The substance will be different for each individual, as each person has their own need. It is expected that each person will have their own faith in God, since they know what they want God to do for them. Faith brings the impossible to possible, since people are already visualizing what they expect to have for the future.
Things	The word "things" represents anything that persons will believe God for. Some persons may believe God for a vehicle, while others believe God for children, for companions, for a change of government, etc. The word "things" is used in its plural form. Therefore, persons can expect many things from God, since there is no limitation of their expectations of the Creator. God is never distracted when persons ask him for many things, since he has the ability to give many things to those who ask of him. The word "things" has no restriction on the size of the things that people are believing God for. For example, one person can ask God for a 5% increase in their salary, while another person can ask God to make them the ruler of a great city.

Hoped	Each individual must have belief in whatever they need from God. They must be willing to exercise some physical and mental energy as they expect God to answer their request. Because faith is futuristic, it requires a person to think and expect things to happen some time in the near future.
Evidence	People do not have evidence before they pray, but they have a mental picture of what their evidence will look like. This therefore means that they have a prototype of what they are expecting from God. If they do not imagine the evidence of what they are praying for, how will they know that their faith has materialized?
Things	While the word "things" is used twice in this short sentence that provides the definition of faith, there is purpose in stating it twice. On the first occasion, people can ask anything from God; however, they must not waver in their faith. Therefore, whatever they ask of God, they must know that he will do the same thing for them. For example, if a person asks God to pass an examination, but they expect to fail the examination, then they are saying one thing and expecting a different result. Their faith must be consistent with what they want to see happen, and they must not change their belief, even when many things may not look possible. Believers must not change their belief in God when external things change. Faith is like having a one-track mindset, where the believer expects only one result and does not change their belief. So, whatever they ask for, that is the only thing that they are expecting to see happen.

Not seen	Faith always moves the possibility of things happening from the believer's mind into the hands of God. When persons are exercising faith, they never have the evidence. They cannot touch their evidence. Their evidence is always in the future. When people see the results, then they do not need to exercise faith. Therefore, they will exercise faith for those things which are not available to them right now, but which they want God to do for them.

2.2 Is faith necessary?

Yes, faith is necessary, since a person cannot serve God without faith. Hebrews 11:6 tells us that persons cannot receive anything from God without faith. Faith causes people to think of tomorrow and see a brighter future, even when they are having difficult days.

Hebrews 11:6

6 But without faith it is impossible to please him: for he that cometh to God must believe that he is, and that he is a rewarder of them that diligently seek him.

3. Double-mindedness affects faith

Believers sometimes operate as though they are not sure what they need from God. They have a situation, and today they ask God to address the situation in a specific way. Tomorrow they approach God concerning the same situation, but this time around, they ask him to address it differently, and the next day they pray a different prayer for the same situation. God is never confused, so believers must know what they need and stick with it (James 1:8).

Constantly changing your request to God can delay or even prevent your prayers from being answered. When believers want to pray, they first must know what they need from God, then think carefully about what their needs are, and then make it a matter of prayer (Hebrews 11:6).

Sometimes, external factors can cause believers to think many things, but they must not change their focus on what they need to see God do for them.

James 1:2-8

²My brethren, count it all joy when ye fall into divers temptations; ³Knowing this, that the trying of your faith worketh patience. ⁴But let patience have her perfect work, that ye may be perfect and entire, wanting nothing. ⁵If any of you lack wisdom, let him ask of God, that giveth to all men liberally, and upbraideth not; and it shall be given him. ⁶But let him ask in faith, nothing wavering. For he that wavereth is like a wave of the sea driven with the wind and tossed. ⁷For let not that man think that he shall receive any thing of the Lord. ⁸A double minded man is unstable in all his ways.

3.1 Remain focused with your request to God

Remember that with faith, people do not have the results, so they need to make a specific request to God and expect him to answer that which they ask of him. Therefore, if they keep changing their expectation, it will appear that they do not know what they needed in the first place.

Consider this example. A child approaches his parents two months before his twentieth birthday and asks them to purchase a new blue car. The following month, the child asks his parents to purchase a red car. Two weeks before his birthday, he changes his request again and asks his parents to purchase a Sport Utility Vehicle (SUV) for him instead of the car.

It appears that the child does not know what he really needs for his twentieth birthday, since he changed from a new blue car to a red car to an SUV. Many believers often do a similar thing to God, and when their prayers are not answered, they blame him.

When Hannah prayed to God in 1 Samuel 1:9-21 (see chapter 9), she knew that she needed a male child, and she did not change her request. She set a good example for believers to be consistent in their prayer request to God.

Consider another example. In this case, a believer is trusting God to move from a rented house to their own home. They choose to pray about the matter and ask God to help them to construct a two-story house within a two-year duration. Subsequently, the believer approaches God and tells God their relationship with their landlord is better and they no longer need to build the two-story house, but they need money to purchase a van.

If God did not answer this believer's request to assist them with providing the finances to build their house, do you think that he is God? Well, based upon your knowledge of God, please help believers to remain focused and not be double-minded, since if they are, their prayers will not be answered by God.

3.2 Your faith will be tested

The faith of every believer will be tested, according to James 1:2-4. However, when believers' faith is tested, they must remain focused. They must become patient. Patience is one of the things that many persons appear to lack. They believe that everything they need must be given to them immediately. But there are times when God is observing them before he answers their prayer.

Figure 2. When faith is tried, it produces patience

Whenever your faith is tested, do not change your relationship with God. Do not change your desire for God. Do not change your request to God.

Whenever you are going through difficult situations, do not quit being that person whom the Lord called you to be. Continue to serve the Lord faithfully and be a blessing to others.

If you ask God to increase your wisdom, then do not change your request. If you ask God to make you a great worshipper, then remain focused with your prayer.

4. You cannot serve God without faith

There are many persons who may be thinking that they do not have to have faith to serve God, but they are all wrong. God wants believers to live by faith. The just shall live by faith and not by their own imagination.

Romans 1:17

17 For therein is the righteousness of God revealed from faith to faith: as it is written, The just shall live by faith.

Everyone who needs God and his blessings needs faith. It is impossible to please God without faith.

Hebrews 11:6

6 But without faith it is impossible to please him: for he that cometh to God must believe that he is, and that he is a rewarder of them that diligently seek him.

It is now important to analyze the latter part of Hebrews 11:6 into two main parts; that is, "believe that he is" and "that he is a rewarder."

4.1 Believe that he is

If a person does not believe that God is God, then they are wasting their time in asking him anything. They must first conceptualize that they are asking the God who can make all things possible.

Moses had an interaction with God, and he wanted to know how to describe God to the Egyptians. He presented an intelligent question to God and expected that God would provide the answer, which he would then use to convince the people of who God is. However, God answered Moses, but the answer Moses received did not provide him with as much clarity as he might have anticipated.

Exodus 3:13-15

13 And Moses said unto God, Behold, when I come unto the children of Israel, and shall say unto them, The God of your fathers hath sent me unto you; and they shall say to me, What is his name? what shall I say unto them? 14 And

God said unto Moses, I AM THAT I AM: and he said, Thus shalt thou say unto the children of Israel, I AM hath sent me unto you. 15 And God said moreover unto Moses, Thus shalt thou say unto the children of Israel, the LORD God of your fathers, the God of Abraham, the God of Isaac, and the God of Jacob, hath sent me unto you: this is my name for ever, and this is my memorial unto all generations.

4.2 Believe that he is a rewarder

Remember that those who will serve God and want anything from him must first believe in him. Once they believe in him and ask anything of him, then they can expect that he will reward them. It must be known that God has the power and ability to reward anyone who believes in him. When a child approaches their parents and asks them for something, that child must assess if their parents can reward them with whatever they ask for. Whenever believers approach God, they must believe that God can reward them with whatever they ask of him.

Luke 11:11-13

11 If a son shall ask bread of any of you that is a father, will he give him a stone? or if he ask a fish, will he for a fish give him a serpent? 12 Or if he shall ask an egg, will he offer him a scorpion? 13 If ye then, being evil, know how to give good gifts unto your children: how much more shall your heavenly Father give the Holy Spirit to them that ask him?

Jesus taught an important lesson to the disciples in Luke 11:11-13. He reminded them that if they ask their heavenly Father for something, then he will not do something different from that which they ask. He likened his example to a relationship between a father and a son.

Take note that it is God's desire to load his children with blessings daily. Therefore, after what he did for his children yesterday, he wants to do something new for them today.

Psalm 68:19

19 Blessed be the Lord, who daily loadeth us with benefits, even the God of our salvation. Selah.

5. Saved by faith

Anyone who knows Jesus as Lord and Savior will only know him through faith. Persons sometimes believe that their works will save them, but for anyone to get into the kingdom of God, they need to go through Jesus.

5.1 Born a sinner

No one was born without sin, even if their parents were believers. If children were raised in Christian homes, that will not save them, since they were born sinners and must individually confess their sins unto the Lord.

Romans 3:23

23 For all have sinned, and come short of the glory of God.

5.2 Sin has a price

The Apostle Paul was clear in his writing that the payment for sin is death. This therefore means that everyone should have been dead because of their sins.

Romans 6:23

23 For the wages of sin is death; but the gift of God is eternal life through Jesus Christ our Lord.

Jesus stated that if people do not repent, they will die.

Luke 13:5

5 I tell you, Nay: but, except ye repent, ye shall all likewise perish.

5.3 Salvation through faith, not works

There is only one way out of sin, and that is to accept Jesus. Even those who are rich and famous cannot save themselves. The works of great men and women will not save them. Everyone needs to accept Jesus through faith if they want to be saved.

Ephesians 2:8-10

8 For by grace are ye saved through faith; and that not of yourselves: it is the gift of God: 9 Not of works, lest any man should boast. 10 For we are his workmanship, created in Christ Jesus unto good works, which God hath before ordained that we should walk in them.

The law cannot save anyone, so persons must not measure their works against the law to justify whether they can make it into the kingdom of God.

Romans 3:28

28 Therefore we conclude that a man is justified by faith without the deeds of the law.

6. Activate your faith through God's Word

People can do many things to stir their faith. However, there is one thing that they should do very often as they stay focused on God.

Romans 10:14-17

14 How then shall they call on him in whom they have not believed? and how shall they believe in him of whom they have not heard? and how shall they hear without a preacher? 15 And how shall they preach, except they be sent? as it is written, How beautiful are the feet of them that preach the gospel of peace, and bring glad tidings of good things! 16 But they have not all obeyed the gospel. For Esaias saith, Lord, who hath believed our report? 17 So then faith cometh by hearing, and hearing by the word of God.

Preaching of God's Word is not the only thing people need in order to believe in God. However, when God's Word is shared with them through preaching, teaching, and evangelism, they are reminded of God's truth and they begin to believe God's Word.

6.1 Preach and teach God's Word

Those who are called to preach, teach, and evangelize must not try to present their own truth, but God's truth. Some religious leaders believe that they are doing God a favor when they present information that sounds enticing but is not consistent with God's Word. Leaders must resist the temptation of trying to make great names for themselves and instead think of showcasing God's greatness.

In his *Illustrated Bible Dictionary* (1894, 250), Matthew George Easton provides this definition of faith:

Faith is the result of teaching (Rom 10:14-17). Knowledge is an essential element in all faith, and is sometimes spoken of as an equivalent to faith (John 10:38; 1 John 2:3). Yet the two are distinguished in this respect, that faith includes in it assent, which is an act of the will in addition to the act of the understanding. Assent to the truth is of the essence of faith, and the ultimate ground on which our assent to any revealed truth rests is the veracity of God.

6.2 God's Word ignites the flame of faith

As people hear the Word of God, it ignites a flame in them. They become energized and believe in God to do the impossible. That all becomes possible, since those who hear God's Word have a better understanding of who God is and how many great things he has in store for them.

For example, when a school teacher sits down and explains to students that if they study for their examinations and are successful, many opportunities will become possible for them, then those students will be motivated to pass their examinations. Many students have careers that they want to get into, but they must first finish their examinations. Therefore, standing between them and their career choice is their teacher and the examination.

A similar thing happens to believers: they want great success, but they must first put faith in God. Many believers need teachers and preachers of God's Word to let them know that great things will happen for them if they only trust God for whatever they would like to see in the future.

Figure 3. Influence of school teachers and preachers on the lives of their listeners

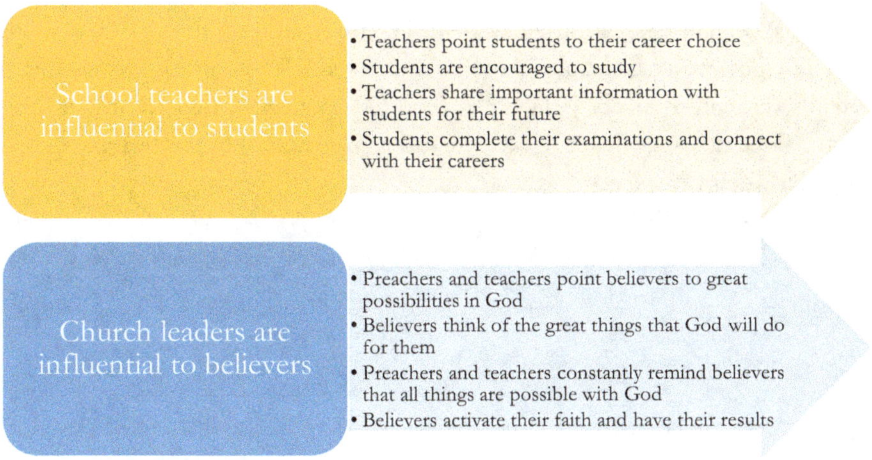

6.3 He magnifies his Word above his name

The Psalmist was clear to state that God magnifies his Word above his name, according to Psalm 138:2. So, those who need to strengthen their faith must know God's Word and believe him more and more.

Psalm 138:1-3

2 I will worship toward thy holy temple, and praise thy name for thy lovingkindness and for thy truth: for thou hast magnified thy word above all thy name.

6.4 Meditate on God's Word

Persons sometimes operate as though they are in a hurry to read God's Word and then leave the scriptures at home or at church. However, when persons hear God's Word, they have personal responsibilities to meditate on it, since they have to activate their faith.

Joshua 1:8

8 This book of the law shall not depart out of thy mouth; but thou shalt meditate therein day and night, that thou mayest observe to do according to all that is written therein: for then thou shalt make thy way prosperous, and then thou shalt have good success.

6.5 Where to hide God's Word

In some communities and countries, persons are not allowed to carry their Bibles. Also, at some workplaces, believers are occupied with their work and will not get the opportunity to read the Word of God during their lunch breaks. However, every believer is required to keep God's Word in their heart, since no one can see it. No one can charge believers for carrying God's Word in their hearts.

Psalm 119:11

11 Thy word have I hid in mine heart, that I might not sin against thee.

Figure 4. The resting place of God's Word for the believer

Many persons attend regular church services and Bible studies to hear God's Word, but they must make a deliberate attempt to move the Word of God from the Bible to their hearts. When God's words are in the hearts of believers, then those believers will be quick to respond to anything that needs faith to be activated, without having to wait for preachers and teachers of God's Word to stir them.

7. Minimum amount of faith

As Jesus was teaching, he provided useful information not only to those who listened to him on that day, but also to many who read the scriptures now. Many persons today have not seen a mustard seed, which is a very small seed. People may ask, what does a mustard seed have to do with faith? That is a good question, which should be directed to Jesus. In the Gospel of Matthew, Jesus draws a parallel between the mustard seed and the believers' faith.

He challenged believers that if they have faith like a mustard seed, then they can speak to an object as big as a mountain and their little faith will be enough to move it. This may sound strange to many persons, since they expect that it would take one big thing to move another big thing. For example, a crane is needed to lift very heavy metal when there is construction work on high-rise buildings. But Jesus spoke about a small thing, a mustard seed, that can move a big thing such as a mountain.

Matthew 17:20

20 And Jesus said unto them, Because of your unbelief: for verily I say unto you, If ye have faith as a grain of mustard seed, ye shall say unto this mountain, Remove hence to yonder place; and it shall remove; and nothing shall be impossible unto you.

Jesus is not expecting believers to have small faith, but he wants them to know that even if their faith is small, it still has a great impact. For comparison, some persons may ask what can happen if they have a large faith. That is a great question, but it is expected that with more faith, more will be done.

God wants his children's faith to arise. He does not want his children to live in doubt and fail to believe that he can make great things happen for them.

7.1 Nothing is impossible with God

Yes, believers need to hear this once again: nothing is impossible with God. There may be many situations that will confront believers, but they must believe in God as he is working on their behalf.

In Matthew 17:20, Jesus told the disciples that nothing will be impossible unto them. He wants to assure them that they have God on their side, if they only believe in him and exercise their faith.

8. Faith can bring blessings to you

If you are not blessed and need God's blessings, then exercise faith. There are many things that God wants to do for his children, but he wants them to exercise their faith in him, and then he will be there to take care of their needs. Those persons who are faithful to God must expect his blessings to come upon their lives.

Proverbs 28:20

20 A faithful man shall abound with blessings: but he that maketh haste to be rich shall not be innocent.

Many times, evildoers are involved in works that cause many of them to gain temporary material wealth. However, God wants to bless his children beyond today, and he wants his children to know that they will inherit the earth if they remain committed to him.

Psalm 37:7-9

7 Rest in the LORD, and wait patiently for him: fret not thyself because of him who prospereth in his way, because of the man who bringeth wicked devices to pass. 8 Cease from anger, and forsake wrath: fret not thyself in any wise to do evil. 9 For evildoers shall be cut off: but those that wait upon the LORD, they shall inherit the earth.

God has the ability to take his children from whatever difficult situation they are experiencing and bless them. Even when believers are in horrible pits, he can still reach them and rescue them. Therefore, they must continue to wait on him for their blessings and protections.

Psalm 40:1-2

1 I waited patiently for the LORD; and he inclined unto me, and heard my cry. 2 He brought me up also out of an horrible pit, out of the miry clay, and set my feet upon a rock, and established my goings.

Figure 5. Waiting on God for prosperity

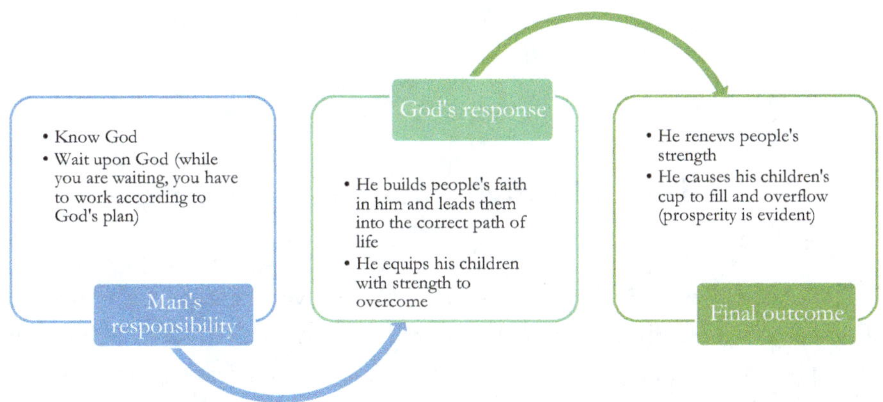

Psalm 104:27-28

27 These wait all upon thee; that thou mayest give them their meat in due season.
28 That thou givest them they gather: thou openest thine hand, they are filled with good.

9. Faith and prayer changes barrenness

The story of Hannah is well known by believers. Hannah was one of Elkanah's wives. She was married, and she wanted a child, just like her counterpart, Peninnah. However, the scripture tells readers that it was God who had shut up Hannah's womb. It may appear impossible to pray to God who had caused her womb to be shut up, but Hannah was not going to back down, since she knew what she needed from God, and she placed her faith in God that he would answer her prayer.

Hannah was precise in her request to God, which enabled her prayer to be answered. Believers should demonstrate a similar attitude to Hannah when they place their faith in God.

1 Samuel 1:9-21

9 So Hannah rose up after they had eaten in Shiloh, and after they had drunk. Now Eli the priest sat upon a seat by a post of the temple of the LORD. 10 And she was in bitterness of soul, and prayed unto the LORD, and wept sore. 11 And she vowed a vow, and said, O LORD of hosts, if thou wilt indeed look on the affliction of thine handmaid, and remember me, and not forget thine handmaid, but wilt give unto thine handmaid a man child, then I will give him unto the LORD all the days of his life, and there shall no razor come upon his head.

12 And it came to pass, as she continued praying before the LORD, that Eli marked her mouth. 13 Now Hannah, she spake in her heart; only her lips moved, but her voice was not heard: therefore Eli thought she had been drunken. 14 And Eli said unto her, How long wilt thou be drunken? put away thy wine from thee. 15 And Hannah answered and said, No, my lord, I am a woman of a sorrowful spirit: I have drunk neither wine nor strong drink, but have poured out my soul before the LORD. 16 Count not thine handmaid for a daughter of Belial: for out of the abundance of my complaint and grief have I spoken hitherto. 17 Then Eli answered and said, Go in peace: and the God of Israel grant thee thy petition that thou hast asked of him. 18 And she said, Let thine handmaid find grace in thy sight. So the woman went her way, and did eat, and her countenance was no more sad.

¹⁹ And they rose up in the morning early, and worshipped before the LORD, and returned, and came to their house to Ramah: and Elkanah knew Hannah his wife; and the LORD remembered her. ²⁰ Wherefore it came to pass, when the time was come about after Hannah had conceived, that she bare a son, and called his name Samuel, saying, Because I have asked him of the LORD. ²¹ And the man Elkanah, and all his house, went up to offer unto the LORD the yearly sacrifice, and his vow.

Figure 6. Things to note about Hannah's faith and prayer

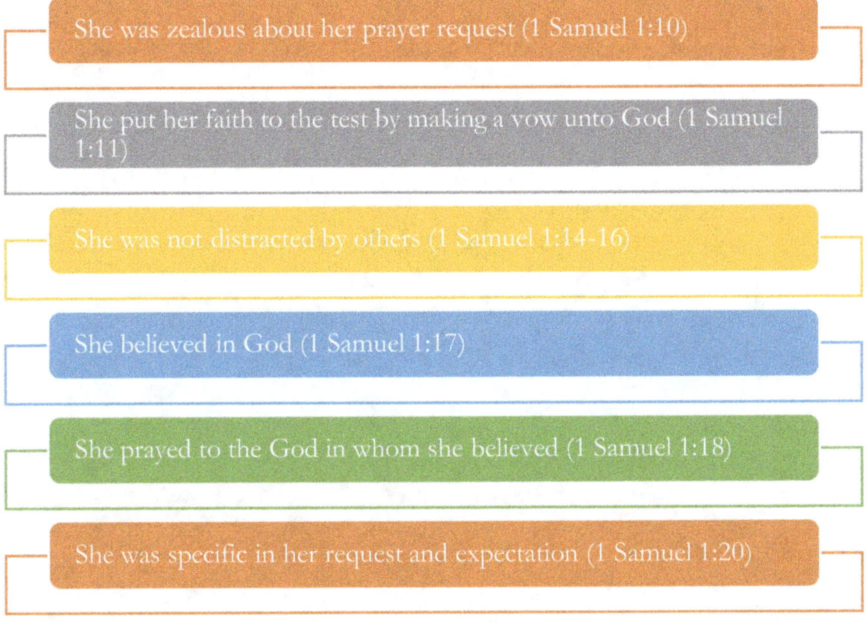

If God had given Hannah a girl child, she would have been disappointed, but she was specific in her request to God and asked him for a male child. Take note, while Hannah prayed and had faith in God, she had to do her natural part in life. It is clear that after her prayer, she had intimate relations with her husband according to 1 Samuel 1:19. If she had slept with a strange man, then she could not have expected God to fulfill her prayer. Hannah did not deviate in her prayer. Too many believers want God to do great things for them, but they fail to do the human part of life. Faith requires action from people. Faith without works is dead.

Believers are sometimes guilty of only praying, but not doing their part. Therefore, many of them are without any results unto this day.

Hannah was not asking God for something bad, so she placed faith in that which she needed. She did not complain to other persons about her barrenness, but she built up her faith and approached God about it, since it is only he who had the ability to cause her to bring forth a child.

If Hannah prayed against something that God had caused to happen to her, then you can do the same thing today. If God was willing to change his decision about King Hezekiah and added more years to him, then you must also have faith in God.

10. Exercise great faith for healing

There was a centurion whose servant was sick. This centurion cared very much about his servant. This is the care that many leaders need to have towards those who work honestly for them.

Most parents will know that if their child is sick, it is like they are also sick. Because of the love parents have for their children, they are often willing to do anything to allow their children to be healed.

These are some examples of what parents have done when their children are sick:

- Stop working to care for their children
- Sell some of their assets to pay their children's medical bills
- Change jobs just to have more time to look after their children
- Seek financial help from families, friends, and even strangers
- Host fundraisers to finance their children's medical expenses
- Take their children to the most expensive medical institutions and doctors to seek help for them
- Ask other parents what they did when their children had similar illness and how those illnesses were healed

Children sometimes do not know the challenges that their parents go through for them. It is expected that children will appreciate their parents and try to be supportive to them, since many parents will not tell their children of all of the sacrifices they have made for them.

The centurion wanted to go home with victory, knowing that his servant was healed, so he approached Jesus to heal his servant. He had to put his faith in Jesus, the healer. If the centurion did not believe, then he would have wasted his time approaching Jesus. However, not only did he believe that Jesus would heal his servant, he also believed that Jesus could speak the word from wherever he was, and that was sufficient for his servant's healing. This man exercised great faith.

Take note, the centurion approached Jesus and told Jesus how the healing could be done. He had great faith and believed that once faith is in the equation, there is no barrier that can stop prayer. He asked Jesus just to speak the word.

Matthew 8:5-13

⁵And when Jesus was entered into Capernaum, there came unto him a centurion, beseeching him, ⁶And saying, Lord, my servant lieth at home sick of the palsy, grievously tormented. ⁷And Jesus saith unto him, I will come and heal him. ⁸The centurion answered and said, Lord, I am not worthy that thou shouldest come under my roof: but speak the word only, and my servant shall be healed. ⁹For I am a man under authority, having soldiers under me: and I say to this man, Go, and he goeth; and to another, Come, and he cometh; and to my servant, Do this, and he doeth it.

¹⁰When Jesus heard it, he marvelled, and said to them that followed, Verily I say unto you, I have not found so great faith, no, not in Israel. ¹¹And I say unto you, That many shall come from the east and west, and shall sit down with Abraham, and Isaac, and Jacob, in the kingdom of heaven. ¹²But the children of the kingdom shall be cast out into outer darkness: there shall be weeping and gnashing of teeth. ¹³And Jesus said unto the centurion, Go thy way; and as thou hast believed, so be it done unto thee. And his servant was healed in the selfsame hour.

Jesus told the centurion to go his way, because what the centurion was expecting for his servant had already happened due to his faith. Jesus may wish that more persons will approach him with similar faith.

God wants to make the work very light for many persons, but they must walk with their faith. They must specify what they want God to do for them.

There are some persons who approach God with their status, telling him what positions they occupy. Everyone needs to know that God is not moved by their status, but by their faith. Therefore, they must approach God in humility and believe that he is a rewarder of them that believe in him.

Although the centurion told Jesus of his status, he was quick to let Jesus know that he believed in him and that his purpose for meeting Jesus was for his servant to be healed. Jesus loves when persons are honest with him and avoid trying to impress him with enticing words and their status.

11. Touch him with your faith

Jesus is always interested in people having a better understanding of the word of God and increasing their knowledge of him and his Father. Jesus was teaching, as he loved doing, and many persons approached him and asked questions or wanted him to do something special for them. Jesus remained very kind and would stop what he was doing to meet the needs of many persons, as he was a leader who had the people's interest at heart.

Luke 8:40-48

40 And it came to pass, that, when Jesus was returned, the people gladly received him: for they were all waiting for him. 41 And, behold, there came a man named Jairus, and he was a ruler of the synagogue: and he fell down at Jesus' feet, and besought him that he would come into his house: 42 For he had one only daughter, about twelve years of age, and she lay a dying. But as he went the people thronged him. 43 And a woman having an issue of blood twelve years, which had spent all her living upon physicians, neither could be healed of any, 44 Came behind him, and touched the border of his garment: and immediately her issue of blood stanched. 45 And Jesus said, Who touched me? When all denied, Peter and they that were with him said, Master, the multitude throng thee and press thee, and sayest thou, Who touched me? 46 And Jesus said, Somebody hath touched me: for I perceive that virtue is gone out of me. 47 And when the woman saw that she was not hid, she came trembling, and falling down before him, she declared unto him before all the people for what cause she had touched him, and how she was healed immediately. 48 And he said unto her, Daughter, be of good comfort: thy faith hath made thee whole; go in peace.

11.1 Believe in him

If you are expecting to touch Jesus with your faith, then you have to believe in him. Many persons need things from the Lord, but they do not have a relationship with him. For example, a child may approach their parents and ask them for something. Once the parents have whatever the child asked for and there is no harm in providing what was requested, then the parents will help their child. Take note, it all happens because there is a relationship between parents and child. If a stranger were to come and ask for the same thing, then it might take a long time before the parent would even consider helping a stranger. In some cases, the stranger may be sent away with nothing.

According to Luke 8:44, the woman with the issue of blood came to Jesus and touched him. However, before she left all that she was doing to come and touch him, she had to believe in him. This woman visited many physicians first, and after receiving no help from them, she approached Jesus. She had done her background checks and knew that he was not an ordinary man but one with the power to heal, so she came to him because she believed in him.

11.2 Go after him

After living with a life-threatening health issue for many years, persons need whatever help they can get. They sometimes reach a stage where they are willing to try anything new because they need to be healed.

There were many reasons why this woman could have refused to go after Jesus. Consider these reasons and see how she exercised faith in Jesus:

- Jesus was in the village and many persons were expecting him (verse 40)
- There was a great crowd making much noise as they needed the attention of Jesus, the healer (verse 40)
- Jesus had just been intercepted by Jairus, who needed his daughter to be made whole (verse 41)
- The crowd did not operate in any orderly manner, as they almost crushed Jesus (verse 42)
- This woman had lost much blood and was physically weak (verse 43)
- She was unable to touch him from the front because of the crowd, so she went behind him and touched the edge of his cloak (verse 44).

11.3 Touch him

This woman wanted her healing, and she needed it badly. She could have waited until Jesus had finished speaking to the crowd and healed Jairus's daughter, but she was not going to follow protocol that day. One problem with many believers is that they have too many excuses for why they will not reach out to Jesus. If they take note of this woman, they will see that she put aside all excuses and went to the healer. Many persons may be astonished that she came from behind to touch the edge of his cloak. The disciples were amazed when Jesus asked the question "Who touched me?" Even unto today, many persons would be surprised to know that someone could be going through a crowd where there is no orderly behavior from the people and will stop to ask who touched them.

In rural markets where sellers are vending, those who go to make their purchases may be very close to each other, as many buyers are looking for bargains. Those who can speak in loud tones will get the attention of the buyers and may get some favor. Another example is that at a sporting event where popular athletes will be playing, the crowd may often be unruly, and it may be difficult for some to even hear their own voices, as many persons may be shouting or pushing to get into the place.

With all that was happening around Jesus with the crowd, this woman touched Jesus from behind. He stopped what he was doing and inquired about who touched him. It could not have been this woman's physical touch that caught his attention; rather, it was the virtue that left his body through the faith she exercised. It can be seen through Jesus' earthly ministry that whenever someone touched him with faith, he stopped what he was doing to acknowledge what that person did or bring it to the attention of others. Faith indeed moves God, and whenever someone touches him through faith, he knows, because it causes something to ignite in his body.

From all indication in Luke 8:46, Jesus did not know who physically touched him, but he perceived that virtue had left his body. It is the first time he made such a statement. Therefore, this woman had to exercise faith to such an extent that he was willing to ask who had touched him in faith, because something great was felt in his body.

If believers are willing to touch Jesus through faith in a similar way as what this woman did, then many of their concerns will be addressed. It was not this woman's physical touch that allowed her to be healed, since she was only able to touch the edge of his cloak, but the faith which she exercised.

It is important to note that Jesus never touched this woman. He did not speak with her before she touched him. He did not see her coming, since she came from behind him. If your faith is going to touch Jesus, then you have to press past your limitations and exercise faith in him, who has the ability to do wonders for you. Touch any part of Jesus through faith today and let him meet you at the point of your need. Never let the crowd distract you from reaching Jesus; you need to exercise faith in him, and he will bless you.

12. Friends helping a friend to be healed

When persons are sick, that is when they need much help. Strangely, when some persons are sick, they have fewer friends, as most persons choose not to be at their side. Some people will only be friends with others, because of what they can get from them. But true friends stay through good and bad times, in sickness and in health. Are you a friend that many persons can count on when they are in need?

Examining the scripture in Luke 5:17-26, you will see how some friends were willing to use their faith for their friend to be healed. These friends could have been charged for disturbing Jesus and the people. They also could have been charged for letting their friend down through the top of the building.

Luke 5:17-26

17 And it came to pass on a certain day, as he was teaching, that there were Pharisees and doctors of the law sitting by, which were come out of every town of Galilee, and Judaea, and Jerusalem: and the power of the Lord was present to heal them. 18 And, behold, men brought in a bed a man which was taken with a palsy: and they sought means to bring him in, and to lay him before him. 19 And when they could not find by what way they might bring him in because of the multitude, they went upon the housetop, and let him down through the tiling with his couch into the midst before Jesus. 20 And when he saw their faith, he said unto him, Man, thy sins are forgiven thee. 21 And the scribes and the Pharisees began to reason, saying, Who is this which speaketh blasphemies? Who can forgive sins, but God alone?

22 But when Jesus perceived their thoughts, he answering said unto them, What reason ye in your hearts? 23 Whether is easier, to say, Thy sins be forgiven thee; or to say, Rise up and walk? 24 But that ye may know that the Son of man hath power upon earth to forgive sins, (he said unto the sick of the palsy,) I say unto thee, Arise, and take up thy couch, and go into thine house. 25 And immediately he rose up before them, and took up that whereon he lay, and departed to his own house, glorifying God. 26 And they were all amazed, and they glorified God, and were filled with fear, saying, We have seen strange things to day.

When you are exercising faith in God, do not let anything stand between you and your God. Would you exercise some faith reach out for a friend today who needs healing? You may not be able to let your friend down through the top of the house, but can you take that friend to the hospital and pay some of those medical bills? Can you pray for your friend to be healed? Can you fast for your friend to be healed? Today, do whatever you can to help someone who needs healing. Do not just talk about your faith, but live your faith.

13. Let your faith be counted as righteousness

Abraham was not a perfect man. He was just like any other human, but he had faith in God and it was credited to him as righteousness. If God was willing to work with Abraham and make him and his name great, then God is also willing to work with all believers.

God sent Abraham to a new land. Many leaders would question God about such a request, since they are going to a place they do not know and may be lacking some essential resources, yet Abraham allowed his faith in God to accept God's request, and he went on his journey.

Abraham also took his family with him, as he believed that God had promised to do something great for him. Some persons believe that faith is blind trust in an unknown God. However, Abraham had a relationship with the Lord, and he trusted that God knew what he was doing, so it was his responsibility to trust God and follow wherever he was led. It turned out that God, who is always right, did such great things for Abraham that even unto today, many believers still talk about Abraham and his faith in God.

Romans 4:1-25

1 What shall we say then that Abraham our father, as pertaining to the flesh, hath found? 2 For if Abraham were justified by works, he hath whereof to glory; but not before God. 3 For what saith the scripture? Abraham believed God, and it was counted unto him for righteousness. 4 Now to him that worketh is the reward not reckoned of grace, but of debt. 5 But to him that worketh not, but believeth on him that justifieth the ungodly, his faith is counted for righteousness. 6 Even as David also describeth the blessedness of the man, unto whom God imputeth righteousness without works, 7 Saying, Blessed are they whose iniquities are forgiven, and whose sins are covered. 8 Blessed is the man to whom the Lord will not impute sin.

9 Cometh this blessedness then upon the circumcision only, or upon the uncircumcision also? for we say that faith was reckoned to Abraham for righteousness. 10 How was it then reckoned? when he was in circumcision, or in uncircumcision? Not in circumcision, but in uncircumcision. 11 And he received the sign of circumcision, a seal of the righteousness of the faith which he had yet being uncircumcised: that he might be the father of all them that believe, though they be not circumcised; that righteousness might be imputed unto them also: 12 And the father of circumcision to them who are not of the circumcision only, but who also walk in the steps of that faith of our father Abraham, which he had being yet uncircumcised. 13 For the promise, that he should be the heir of the world, was not to Abraham, or to his seed, through the law, but through the righteousness of faith. 14 For if they which are of the law be heirs, faith is made void, and the promise made of none effect: 15 Because the law worketh wrath: for where no law is, there is no transgression.

16 Therefore it is of faith, that it might be by grace; to the end the promise might be sure to all the seed; not to that only which is of the law, but to that also which is of the faith of Abraham; who is the father of us all, 17 (As it is written, I have made thee a father of many nations,) before him whom he believed, even God, who quickeneth the dead, and calleth those things which be not as though they were. 18 Who against hope believed in hope, that he might become the father of many nations, according to that which was spoken, So shall thy seed be. 19 And being not weak in faith, he considered not his own body now dead, when he was about an hundred years old, neither yet the deadness of Sarah's womb: 20 He staggered not at the promise of God through unbelief; but was strong in faith, giving glory to God; 21 And being fully persuaded that, what he had promised, he was able also to perform. 22 And therefore it was imputed to him for righteousness. 23 Now it was not written for his sake alone, that it was imputed to him; 24 But for us also, to whom it shall be imputed, if we believe on him that raised up Jesus our Lord from the dead; 25 Who was delivered for our offences, and was raised again for our justification.

Those who follow God through faith must remember that they have the power to speak to things that do not exist and call those things into being, according to Romans 4:17. Believers have much power available to them, but they must begin to exercise their faith and speak that which they need to see in the future.

14. Faith contributed to the restoration of sight

Another familiar Bible story, this time the one about blind Bartimaeus. He was doing what he knew how to do, because of his infirmity. However, this time around, blind Bartimaeus heard that Jesus was passing his way, and he knew that it was important to get Jesus' attention.

This blind man could have done like many others, allowing Jesus to go about doing the business of his Father without disturbing him. However, Bartimaeus was not prepared to let Jesus pass him without getting his attention. Despite being blind, he was aware that Jesus was not too far from him.

Just imagine Bartimaeus shouting for Jesus while other persons around Jesus were making noise. There was much noise at that time, but Bartimaeus was not going to retreat, since on this day, he was begging not for money, but for his sight.

Mark 10:46-52

46 And they came to Jericho: and as he went out of Jericho with his disciples and a great number of people, blind Bartimaeus, the son of Timaeus, sat by the highway side begging. 47 And when he heard that it was Jesus of Nazareth, he began to cry out, and say, Jesus, thou son of David, have mercy on me. 48 And many charged him that he should hold his peace: but he cried the more a great deal, Thou son of David, have mercy on me. 49 And Jesus stood still, and commanded him to be called. And they call the blind man, saying unto him, Be of good comfort, rise; he calleth thee. 50 And he, casting away his garment, rose, and came to Jesus. 51 And Jesus answered and said unto him, What wilt thou that I should do unto thee? The blind man said unto him, Lord, that I might receive my sight. 52 And Jesus said unto him, Go thy way; thy faith hath made thee whole. And immediately he received his sight, and followed Jesus in the way.

Is there someone today who needs something more than money from Jesus, then calls out his name? As Bartimaeus continued to cry louder, he gained the attention of Jesus and Jesus asked for him to come. Take note that

Bartimaeus was blind, but Jesus asked for him to come (Mark 10:49). Strangely, Bartimaeus cast off his garment (Mark 10:50). This tells us that he was expecting Jesus to heal him, and he was not taking his garment with him. He rose up, as he was prepared to meet this Jesus whom he was calling upon.

When Jesus asked Bartimaeus what he needed from the master, he was quick to state his need. After listening to Bartimaeus, Jesus responded that his faith had made him whole (Mark 10:52). Thus, through faith, Bartimaeus received his sight. There was no need for Jesus to spend much time with him, as his faith was sufficient for his healing.

Jesus had so many unique ways of healing people. For many of them, he did not touch them to make them whole, since they touched him through their faith. Therefore, if you are able to get Jesus' attention and you believe, then whatever situation you are going through, the Lord can heal you. Exercise your faith and claim your healing from the Lord.

15. From the pavilion to the podium

Those who are only spectators cannot receive the blessing of God, since God wants participants and not onlookers. He wants every participant to exercise their faith in him. God is not going to do anything great until his people are willing to invite him and allow him to do the impossible.

What are you believing God for today that is outside of your power? Rest assured that God can meet your needs, if you believe in him and allow him to reign in your life.

Many persons have referred to Hebrews chapter 11 as the "hall of fame" or the "hall of faith." However, it is important to read it once again and see that these were ordinary persons like you and me. Many of them were in the pavilion looking on, but they believed in God, let their faith arise, and moved from the pavilion to the podium. Faith has the ability to transform and transpose persons. If you are in the pavilion, then read Hebrews 11 and know that your name can also be mentioned among many great persons. These were persons with human shortcomings, but they put faith in God, and their names are mentioned for others to see and know their contributions.

Hebrews 11: 1-40

1 Now faith is the substance of things hoped for, the evidence of things not seen. 2 For by it the elders obtained a good report. 3 Through faith we understand that the worlds were framed by the word of God, so that things which are seen were not made of things which do appear. 4 By faith Abel offered unto God a more excellent sacrifice than Cain, by which he obtained witness that he was righteous, God testifying of his gifts: and by it he being dead yet speaketh. 5 By faith Enoch was translated that he should not see death; and was not found, because God had translated him: for before his translation he had this testimony, that he pleased God. 6 But without faith it is impossible to please him: for he that cometh to God must believe that he is, and that he is a rewarder of them that diligently seek him. 7 By faith Noah, being warned of God of things not seen as yet, moved with fear, prepared an ark to the saving of his house; by the which he condemned the world, and became heir of the righteousness which is by faith.

⁸ By faith Abraham, when he was called to go out into a place which he should after receive for an inheritance, obeyed; and he went out, not knowing whither he went. ⁹ By faith he sojourned in the land of promise, as in a strange country, dwelling in tabernacles with Isaac and Jacob, the heirs with him of the same promise: ¹⁰ For he looked for a city which hath foundations, whose builder and maker is God. ¹¹ Through faith also Sara herself received strength to conceive seed, and was delivered of a child when she was past age, because she judged him faithful who had promised. ¹² Therefore sprang there even of one, and him as good as dead, so many as the stars of the sky in multitude, and as the sand which is by the sea shore innumerable.

¹³ These all died in faith, not having received the promises, but having seen them afar off, and were persuaded of them, and embraced them, and confessed that they were strangers and pilgrims on the earth. ¹⁴ For they that say such things declare plainly that they seek a country. ¹⁵ And truly, if they had been mindful of that country from whence they came out, they might have had opportunity to have returned. ¹⁶ But now they desire a better country, that is, an heavenly: wherefore God is not ashamed to be called their God: for he hath prepared for them a city. ¹⁷ By faith Abraham, when he was tried, offered up Isaac: and he that had received the promises offered up his only begotten son, ¹⁸ Of whom it was said, That in Isaac shall thy seed be called: ¹⁹ Accounting that God was able to raise him up, even from the dead; from whence also he received him in a figure. ²⁰ By faith Isaac blessed Jacob and Esau concerning things to come. ²¹ By faith Jacob, when he was a dying, blessed both the sons of Joseph; and worshipped, leaning upon the top of his staff. ²² By faith Joseph, when he died, made mention of the departing of the children of Israel; and gave commandment concerning his bones. ²³ By faith Moses, when he was born, was hid three months of his parents, because they saw he was a proper child; and they were not afraid of the king's commandment. ²⁴ By faith Moses, when he was come to years, refused to be called the son of Pharaoh's daughter; ²⁵ Choosing rather to suffer affliction with the people of God, than to enjoy the pleasures of sin for a season; ²⁶ Esteeming the reproach of Christ greater riches than the treasures in Egypt: for he had respect unto the recompence of the reward. ²⁷ By faith he forsook Egypt, not fearing the wrath of the king: for he endured, as seeing him who is invisible. ²⁸ Through faith he kept the passover, and the sprinkling of blood, lest he that destroyed the firstborn should touch them. ²⁹ By faith they passed through the Red sea as by dry land: which the Egyptians assaying to do were drowned. 30 By faith the walls of Jericho fell down, after they were compassed about seven days. 31 By faith the harlot Rahab perished not with them that believed not, when she had received the spies with peace.

32 And what shall I more say? for the time would fail me to tell of Gedeon, and of Barak, and of Samson, and of Jephthae; of David also, and Samuel, and of the prophets: 33 Who through faith subdued kingdoms, wrought righteousness, obtained promises, stopped the mouths of lions. 34 Quenched the violence of fire, escaped the edge of the sword, out of weakness were made strong, waxed valiant in fight, turned to flight the armies of the aliens. 35 Women received their dead raised to life again: and others were tortured, not accepting deliverance; that they might obtain a better resurrection: 36 And others had trial of cruel mockings and scourgings, yea, moreover of bonds and imprisonment: 37 They were stoned, they were sawn asunder, were tempted, were slain with the sword: they wandered about in sheepskins and goatskins; being destitute, afflicted, tormented; 38 (Of whom the world was not worthy:) they wandered in deserts, and in mountains, and in dens and caves of the earth. 39 And these all, having obtained a good report through faith, received not the promise: 40 God having provided some better thing for us, that they without us should not be made perfect.

As you carefully examine the lives of these individuals mentioned in Hebrews chapter 11, you will notice that they made mistakes like everyone else. If it were not for God's love and forgiveness, they would have died and been forgotten, but while they were alive, they served God by faith, despite never seeing him. Many of these persons followed God because of what they saw and heard of what the Lord did.

Figure 7. Moving from the pavilion to the podium

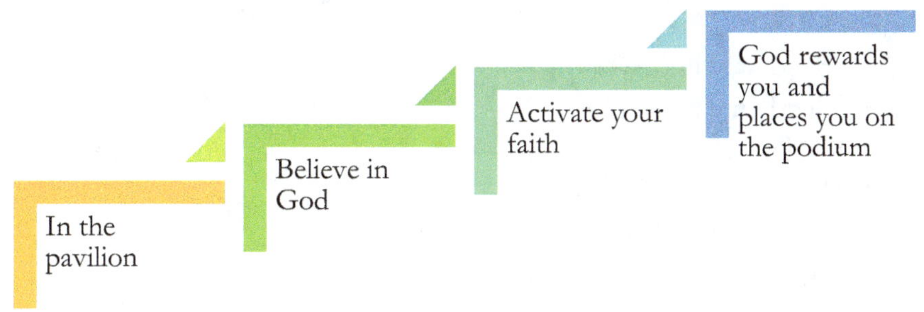

16. Build your faith

Faith is not static, but active. Therefore, faith can be built up.,

16.1 Take personal responsibility to build your faith

Too many times, believers are waiting for others to build up their faith for them. Believers must take personal responsibility to build up their faith.

If a person wants to be healthy, should they wait for their doctor to give them food to eat? When a person has a vehicle, do they expect it to go to the mechanic by itself? Just as one must take the time to take a bath daily, they must also take responsibility to allow their faith to grow in God.

Whenever a person builds up their faith, they can accomplish many things. God expects believers to know his will and spend time building up their faith.

Jude 20

20 But ye, beloved, building up yourselves on your most holy faith, praying in the Holy Ghost.

16.2 How to build up your faith in God

If you are going to build up your faith, then you need to know what to do. These are some of things that every believer ought to do to build up their faith:

- Spend time in prayer
- Spend time in fasting
- Read God's Word
- Mediate on God's Word
- Listen to good preaching and teaching
- Stay quiet in God's presence until he blesses you
- Forgive persons of their sins
- Forgive yourself of past mistakes
- Share the gospel with others

- Listen to gospel songs
- Participate in worship
- Visit persons who are sick and pray for them
- Share your testimonies with others about what the Lord has done for you

16.3 Benefits of building your faith in God

When a person builds their faith, they are doing something good for themselves and others. Therefore, every believer must make it their responsibility to build their faith. These are some benefits when your faith is built:

- You hear directly from God
- Your hear from God more often
- Prayers are answered more quickly than before
- The sick will be healed when you pray for them
- Your worship life will attract God's presence and people will see God in you
- More demons will attack you, but you will be victorious as you stay in God
- You will be encouraged to take on more challenges for God

16.4 Spiritual gift of faith

Every believer ought to ask God for the spiritual gift of faith. You cannot purchase it; it is available to those who will ask.

1 Corinthians 12:9

9 To another faith by the same Spirit; to another the gifts of healing by the same Spirit.

There are some believers who are walking with this spiritual gift but are not aware of it. They thought that their faith had increased because of the years they have spent with the Lord, but it is the Holy Spirit which has come upon them and blessed them with the spiritual gift of faith.

17. Walking in faith

Since faith requires the active participation of people, then they must be doing something for God. Those who walk in faith will constantly see the hands of God at work in and through their lives.

17.1 Believe God and help others

Persons sometimes want to impress others with how good they are and what faithful servants of God they are. The Lord wants to see more persons demonstrate their faith, not only to him, but also to those people who live on this earth with them.

There are some believers who believe that whatever they do, it must only be done to benefit God. However, God has people on the earth to whom he expects every believer to show love and kindness.

James 2:14-26

14 What doth it profit, my brethren, though a man say he hath faith, and have not works? can faith save him? 15 If a brother or sister be naked, and destitute of daily food, 16 And one of you say unto them, Depart in peace, be ye warmed and filled; notwithstanding ye give them not those things which are needful to the body; what doth it profit? 17 Even so faith, if it hath not works, is dead, being alone.

18 Yea, a man may say, Thou hast faith, and I have works: shew me thy faith without thy works, and I will shew thee my faith by my works. 19 Thou believest that there is one God; thou doest well: the devils also believe, and tremble. 20 But wilt thou know, O vain man, that faith without works is dead?

21 Was not Abraham our father justified by works, when he had offered Isaac his son upon the altar? 22 Seest thou how faith wrought with his works, and by works was faith made perfect? 23 And the scripture was fulfilled which saith, Abraham believed God, and it was imputed unto him for righteousness: and he was called the Friend of God. 24 Ye see then how that by works a man is justified, and not by faith only. 25 Likewise also was not Rahab the harlot justified by works, when she had received the messengers, and had sent them out another way? 26 For as the body without the spirit is dead, so faith without works is dead also.

Rahab was living an ungodly life, but she was willing to provide and protect the men of God. Her work to protect God's people was noticed by the Lord, and in return, the Lord saved her and her family.

It cannot be overemphasized that faith without works is dead, as stated in James 2:26. So, every believer who constantly sits and does nothing must know that they are not demonstrating faith. God desires that his people will constantly walk in faith.

Figure 8. Living and dead faith according to James 2:14-26

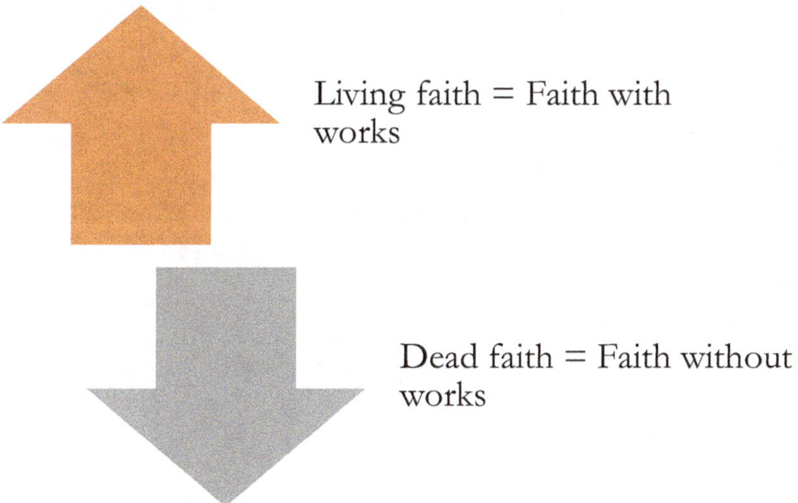

Believers must move away from dead faith and towards living faith. They need to say less and do more. Believers must do things to help both fellow believers and sinners. The attitude and actions shown to sinners may cause them to receive the blessings of God.

17.2 Do not be afraid to shine God's light

Every believer must be willing to demonstrate God in everything they do. They must shine God's light so that the world will see God in them and want to serve the same God.

Matthew 5:15-16

15 Neither do men light a candle, and put it under a bushel, but on a candlestick; and it giveth light unto all that are in the house. 16 Let your light so shine before men, that they may see your good works, and glorify your Father which is in heaven.

Some believers are afraid to let people know that they are saved. However, how can they light their candle and place it under a bushel? Those who are walking in God must do so joyfully and let the world see their faith in God.

17.3 Do the works of God

The Apostle James constantly reminded the believers to be doers of the word. Therefore, persons must first know the word of God, and secondly, they must be willing to become active members of God's army on the earth.

James 1:22

22 But be ye doers of the word, and not hearers only, deceiving your own selves.

17.4 Walk in the Spirit

To fulfill God's work on the earth, believers are reminded to walk in the Spirit and not in the flesh. Those who attempt to walk in the flesh will not fulfill the will of God.

Galatians 5:25

25 If we live in the Spirit, let us also walk in the Spirit.

18. Prayer of faith

There are many persons who are sick. However, those who are strong in the faith are expected to pray that those who are sick will recover. When those who are strong pray for the weak, they must pray in faith, believing that God will heal those for whom they pray.

James 5:13-16

13 Is any among you afflicted? let him pray. Is any merry? let him sing psalms. 14 Is any sick among you? let him call for the elders of the church; and let them pray over him, anointing him with oil in the name of the Lord: 15 And the prayer of faith shall save the sick, and the Lord shall raise him up; and if he have committed sins, they shall be forgiven him. 16 Confess your faults one to another, and pray one for another, that ye may be healed. The effectual fervent prayer of a righteous man availeth much.

Every believer must be willing to exercise their faith when they are praying.

18.1 Why believers must exercise faith when they are praying

Believers can choose not to exercise their faith, but they will not see any positive result. Therefore, why must believers exercise their faith when they are praying?

- They believe that God is their healer
- They transfer their reliance to God
- They place their expectation at the feet of the Lord

19. Be willing to wait

Waiting is something that persons must learn to do. As you travel daily on the roadways, you will experience that many drivers do not want to wait a few seconds for pedestrians to pass. If there is a buildup of traffic, some drivers quickly look for another route, or they may want to overtake other vehicles. When disembarking from a plane, some persons are quick to rush to get their luggage clear through the airport. Those who visit the bank to do a transaction in person often do not want to wait in any line.

While each of us may be in a hurry sometimes, it appears that some persons are almost always in a hurry. Life requires people to exercise patience. Waiting is not a bad thing, and if persons wait, they may save themselves from destruction.

God requires that his children learn to wait. It is not because he cannot deliver their needs, but he sometimes assesses them before responding to their request.

Believers must make their request known unto God and allow him to respond to their request. In the meantime, believers must water their prayer with praise. They must continue to praise the Lord and stop complaining about life.

Philippians 4:6-7

6 Be careful for nothing; but in every thing by prayer and supplication with thanksgiving let your requests be made known unto God. 7 And the peace of God, which passeth all understanding, shall keep your hearts and minds through Christ Jesus.

Apostle Paul cautions believers not to be anxious for anything. He is correct in his admonishments to believers, because many believers do not want to wait.

19.1 Waiting causes strength to be renewed

God wants to renew the strength of his children. However, he wants them to wait on him and not in their own strength. He does not want them to be fretting, but to stay focused on him.

Isaiah 40:31

31 But they that wait upon the LORD shall renew their strength; they shall mount up with wings as eagles; they shall run, and not be weary; and they shall walk, and not faint.

Figure 9. Benefits of waiting on God according to Isaiah 40:31

the benefits mentioned above, why are believers trying to run ahead of God? They need to wait on God and let him place their enemies under their feet. They need to wait upon God until he blesses them.

Believers must not be lackadaisical, but stay with God. Waiting and not doing anything will not produce results. Those who wait must wait in God and not in their own strength. Those who wait in their own strength will fail.

19.2 Waiting on God brings promotion

Joseph was a servant of God. He was placed in the house of Potiphar. As he was working for his master, he was accused of trying to rape Potiphar's wife, which was not true, and Joseph was sent to prison. While he was in prison, he kept his focus and faith on God, and he knew that his God would deliver him.

Joseph was in prison for two years (Genesis 41:1). Most persons will know that whenever a person is sent to prison, they are not entitled to great treatment, but Joseph maintained his faith in God while he was in the prison. He did not backslide, but still trusted his God. During this time, Pharaoh had a dream that no one could interpret until he called for Joseph.

Genesis 41:1-42

1 And it came to pass at the end of two full years, that Pharaoh dreamed: and, behold, he stood by the river. 2 And, behold, there came up out of the river seven well favoured kine and fatfleshed; and they fed in a meadow. 3 And, behold, seven other kine came up after them out of the river, ill favoured and leanfleshed; and stood by the other kine upon the brink of the river. 4 And the ill favoured and leanfleshed kine did eat up the seven well favoured and fat kine. So Pharaoh awoke. 5 And he slept and dreamed the second time: and, behold, seven ears of corn came up upon one stalk, rank and good. 6 And, behold, seven thin ears and blasted with the east wind sprung up after them. 7 And the seven thin ears devoured the seven rank and full ears. And Pharaoh awoke, and, behold, it was a dream.

8 And it came to pass in the morning that his spirit was troubled; and he sent and called for all the magicians of Egypt, and all the wise men thereof: and Pharaoh told them his dream, but there was none that could interpret them unto Pharaoh. 9 Then spake the chief butler unto Pharaoh, saying, I do remember my faults this day: 10 Pharaoh was wroth with his servants, and put me in ward in the captain of the guard's house, both me and the chief baker: 11 And we dreamed a dream in one night, I and he; we dreamed each man according to the interpretation of his dream. 12 And there was there with us a young man, an Hebrew, servant to the captain of the guard; and we told him, and he interpreted to us our dreams; to each man according to his dream he did interpret. 13 And it came to pass, as he interpreted to us, so it was; me he restored unto mine office, and him he hanged.

14 Then Pharaoh sent and called Joseph, and they brought him hastily out of the dungeon: and he shaved himself, and changed his raiment, and came in unto Pharaoh. 15 And Pharaoh said unto Joseph, I have dreamed a dream, and there is none that can interpret it: and I have heard say of thee, that thou canst understand a dream to interpret it. 16 And Joseph answered Pharaoh, saying, It is not in me: God shall give Pharaoh an answer of peace.

17 And Pharaoh said unto Joseph, In my dream, behold, I stood upon the bank of the river: 18 And, behold, there came up out of the river seven kine, fatfleshed and well favoured; and they fed in a meadow: 19 And, behold, seven other kine came up after them, poor and very ill favoured and leanfleshed, such as I never saw in all the land of Egypt for badness: 20 And the lean and the ill favoured kine did eat up the first seven fat kine: 21 And when they had eaten them up, it could not be known that they had eaten them; but they were still ill favoured, as at the beginning. So I awoke. 22 And I saw in my dream, and, behold, seven ears came up in one stalk, full and good: 23 And, behold, seven ears, withered, thin, and blasted with the east wind, sprung up after them: 24 And the thin ears devoured the seven good ears: and I told this unto the magicians; but there was none that could declare it to me.

25 And Joseph said unto Pharaoh, The dream of Pharaoh is one: God hath shewed Pharaoh what he is about to do. 26 The seven good kine are seven years; and the seven good ears are seven years: the dream is one. 27 And the seven thin and ill favoured kine that came up after them are seven years; and the seven empty ears blasted with the east wind shall be seven years of famine. 28 This is the thing which I have spoken unto Pharaoh: What God is about to do he sheweth unto Pharaoh. 29 Behold, there come seven years of great plenty throughout all the land of Egypt: 30 And there shall arise after them seven years of famine; and all the plenty shall be forgotten in the land of Egypt; and the famine shall consume the land; 31 And the plenty shall not be known in the land by reason of that famine following; for it shall be very grievous. 32 And for that the dream was doubled unto Pharaoh twice; it is because the thing is established by God, and God will shortly bring it to pass.

33 Now therefore let Pharaoh look out a man discreet and wise, and set him over the land of Egypt. 34 Let Pharaoh do this, and let him appoint officers over the land, and take up the fifth part of the land of Egypt in the seven plenteous years. 35 And let them gather all the food of those good years that come, and lay up corn under the hand of Pharaoh, and let them keep food in the cities. 36 And that food shall be for store to the land against the seven years of famine, which shall be in the land of Egypt; that the land perish not through the famine. 37 And the thing was good in the eyes of Pharaoh, and in the eyes of all his servants.

38 And Pharaoh said unto his servants, Can we find such a one as this is, a man in whom the Spirit of God is? 39 And Pharaoh said unto Joseph, Forasmuch as God hath shewed thee all this, there is none so discreet and wise as thou art: 40 Thou shalt be over my house, and according unto thy word shall all my people be ruled: only in the throne will I be greater than thou. ⁴¹ And Pharaoh said unto Joseph, See, I have set thee over all the land of Egypt. ⁴² And Pharaoh took off his ring from his hand, and put it upon Joseph's hand, and arrayed him in vestures of fine linen, and put a gold chain about his neck.

In Genesis 41:38-42, God used Pharaoh to promote Joseph. If Joseph had turned his back on God, he might have died in prison, but because he stayed with his redeemer, God was willing to work with Joseph to prove to Pharaoh that there is only one true and living God.

Pharaoh was happy that Joseph interpreted his dream. Pharaoh recognized that the spirit of God was on Joseph, which enabled him to interpret the dream.

19.3 Wait and wait on God

People sometimes believe that they are waiting too long on God. However, Psalm 27:14 reminds all believers to wait and wait on God.

Psalm 27:14

¹⁴ Wait on the LORD: be of good courage, and he shall strengthen thine heart: wait, I say, on the LORD.

19.4 God is willing to wait

Many persons believe that God is impatient. However, he is willing to wait. So, if he is willing to wait, then people should learn to wait also.

Isaiah 30:18

¹⁸ And therefore will the LORD wait, that he may be gracious unto you, and therefore will he be exalted, that he may have mercy upon you: for the LORD is a God of judgment: blessed are all they that wait for him.

19.5 God will lift you up when you wait on him

God will lift up his children when they wait on him. He is willing to change their future from bad to good.

Psalm 40:1-2

¹ I waited patiently for the LORD; and he inclined unto me, and heard my cry. ² He brought me up also out of an horrible pit, out of the miry clay, and set my feet upon a rock, and established my goings.

19.6 Wait on God quietly

Do not make too much noise as you wait on God. As you exercise faith, remain calm and let the Lord work on your behalf.

Lamentations 3:25-26

25 The LORD is good unto them that wait for him, to the soul that seeketh him.
26 It is good that a man should both hope and quietly wait for the salvation of the LORD.

20. Waiting for God's prosperity

No one likes to be without money. When some persons are without money, their appearance is very different and they may not want to interact with anyone.

The beautiful thing about God is that he blesses his children with more than money. He looks after the whole needs of man.

Figure 10. Waiting on God for prosperity

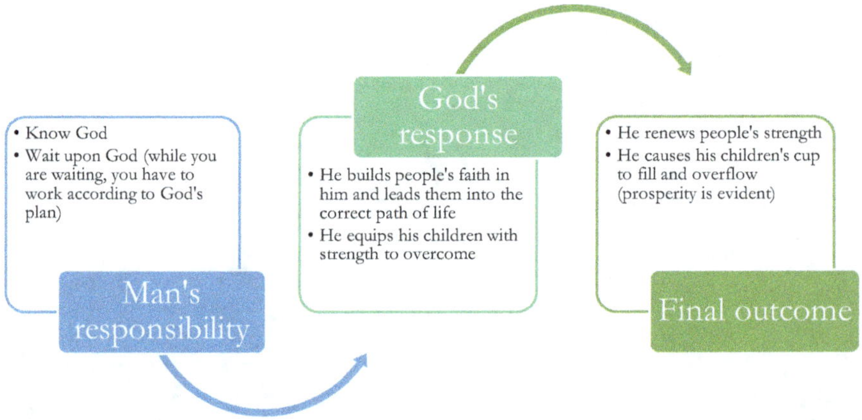

20.1 Do not envy the wicked

Every believer deserves to prosper. However, they must not envy those who are involved in wickedness. Those who do wickedness will have their rewards. God will reward his children and make them prosperous if they wait on him.

For some encouragement to your faith, read Psalm 37. This entire psalm provides reminders to believers to keep trusting God, even when it appears that the wicked are having a great life.

Psalm 37

1 Fret not thyself because of evildoers, neither be thou envious against the workers of iniquity. 2 For they shall soon be cut down like the grass, and wither as the green herb. 3 Trust in the LORD, and do good; so shalt thou dwell in the land, and verily thou shalt be fed. 4 Delight thyself also in the LORD: and he shall give thee the desires of thine heart. 5 Commit thy way unto the LORD; trust also in him; and he shall bring it to pass. 6 And he shall bring forth thy righteousness as the light, and thy judgment as the noonday.

7 Rest in the LORD, and wait patiently for him: fret not thyself because of him who prospereth in his way, because of the man who bringeth wicked devices to pass. 8 Cease from anger, and forsake wrath: fret not thyself in any wise to do evil. 9 For evildoers shall be cut off: but those that wait upon the LORD, they shall inherit the earth. 10 For yet a little while, and the wicked shall not be: yea, thou shalt diligently consider his place, and it shall not be. 11 But the meek shall inherit the earth; and shall delight themselves in the abundance of peace.

12 The wicked plotteth against the just, and gnasheth upon him with his teeth. 13 The LORD shall laugh at him: for he seeth that his day is coming. 14 The wicked have drawn out the sword, and have bent their bow, to cast down the poor and needy, and to slay such as be of upright conversation. 15 Their sword shall enter into their own heart, and their bows shall be broken.

16 A little that a righteous man hath is better than the riches of many wicked. 17 For the arms of the wicked shall be broken: but the LORD upholdeth the righteous. 18 The LORD knoweth the days of the upright: and their inheritance shall be for ever. 19 They shall not be ashamed in the evil time: and in the days of famine they shall be satisfied. 20 But the wicked shall perish, and the enemies of the LORD shall be as the fat of lambs: they shall consume; into smoke shall they consume away.

21 The wicked borroweth, and payeth not again: but the righteous sheweth mercy, and giveth. 22 For such as be blessed of him shall inherit the earth; and they that be cursed of him shall be cut off. 23 The steps of a good man are ordered by the LORD: and he delighteth in his way. 24 Though he fall, he shall not be utterly cast down: for the LORD upholdeth him with his hand.

25 I have been young, and now am old; yet have I not seen the righteous forsaken, nor his seed begging bread. 26 He is ever merciful, and lendeth; and his seed is blessed. 27 Depart from evil, and do good; and dwell for evermore. 28 For the LORD loveth judgment, and forsaketh not his saints; they are preserved for ever: but the seed of the wicked shall be cut off. 29 The righteous shall inherit the land, and dwell therein for ever. 30 The mouth of the righteous speaketh wisdom, and his tongue talketh of judgment. 31 The law of his God is in his heart; none of his steps shall slide. 32 The wicked watcheth the righteous, and seeketh to slay him. 33 The LORD will not leave him in his hand, nor condemn him when he is judged.

34 Wait on the LORD, and keep his way, and he shall exalt thee to inherit the land: when the wicked are cut off, thou shalt see it. 35 I have seen the wicked in great power, and spreading himself like a green bay tree. 36 Yet he passed away, and, lo, he was not: yea, I sought him, but he could not be found. 37 Mark the perfect man, and behold the upright: for the end of that man is peace. 38 But the transgressors shall be destroyed together: the end of the wicked shall be cut off. 39 But the salvation of the righteous is of the LORD: he is their strength in the time of trouble. 40 And the LORD shall help them, and deliver them: he shall deliver them from the wicked, and save them, because they trust in him.

The Psalmist reminds believers to wait on God, as he will exalt them (Psalm 37:34). God is indeed the strength of believers when they are in times of trouble (Psalm 37:39). The Psalmist says that he was young and is now old, yet he has not seen the righteous forsaken, nor his descendants begging bread (Psalm 37:25). This attests to the fact that God provides for his children.

20.2 Daily blessings from God

The God that believers serve wants to bless them daily. Therefore, what they received yesterday is only part of God blessing towards them. God never runs out of things to bless his children. He also blessed them, even when they are not living up to his expectations.

Psalm 68: 19

19 Blessed be the Lord, who daily loadeth us with benefits, even the God of our salvation. Selah.

Psalm 104:27-28

27 These wait all upon thee; that thou mayest give them their meat in due season. 28 That thou givest them they gather: thou openest thine hand, they are filled with good.

21.3 Continue to do good things

Never grow tired of doing the right things. Sometimes, believers can become frustrated with all that is happening around them, but they must remember that they are working unto God and that he expects them to do good things to all people.

Galatians 6:9-10

9 And let us not be weary in well doing: for in due season we shall reap, if we faint not. 10 As we have therefore opportunity, let us do good unto all men, especially unto them who are of the household of faith.

21. Hope in God

God wants every believer to have hope in him that whatever he says, he will bring it to pass. If a person loses hope in God, then there is no faith.

Without knowing God's word, believers will not exercise hope in God. When the external factors look daunting, believers must still have hope in God that he will be there for his children.

Psalm 130:5-6

5 I wait for the LORD, my soul doth wait, and in his word do I hope. 6 My soul waiteth for the Lord more than they that watch for the morning: I say, more than they that watch for the morning.

21.1 Rejoice in hope

People sometimes wait until what they desire comes through before they rejoice. However, as you put faith to work, you should already start to rejoice in hope. Although you have not yet seen the evidence, rejoice in hope because the God you serve will bring it to pass.

Romans 12:12

12 Rejoicing in hope; patient in tribulation; continuing instant in prayer.

When believers pray and hope according to God's word, they must remember that God honors his word and will bring it to pass. That is why believers must know the word of the Lord for themselves, so whatever they ask of God in faith, they can expect that he will do it for them.

Jeremiah 29:11

11 For I know the thoughts that I think toward you, saith the LORD, thoughts of peace, and not of evil, to give you an expected end.

21.2 God of hope

While people know that the Lord is their Savior, many also know him as the God of hope. Therefore, as they place hope in him, he will be there for them, even during their challenging moments.

Romans 15:13

13 Now the God of hope fill you with all joy and peace in believing, that ye may abound in hope, through the power of the Holy Ghost.

21.3 God will not withhold good things from believers

Sometimes, it can be easy to lose your focus on God. As you allow your faith to arise, you must stay with God. Hope in him and him alone. As you remain upright in God, he will be there for you and bless you.

Psalm 84:11

11 For the LORD God is a sun and shield: the LORD will give grace and glory: no good thing will he withhold from them that walk uprightly.

22. Trust in God

The Dake Annotated Reference Bible (1992) provides the Hebrew word for trust: "Batah." It goes on to explain that trust is "to confide in, so as to secure without fear."

As you activate your faith in God, you must trust him to bring things to pass, as he has promised all believers. Sometimes, believers do not know what to expect in the future. They are not sure where to go, but they must move their trust from themselves and place it in God.

Proverbs 3:4-7

4 So shalt thou find favour and good understanding in the sight of God and man. 5 Trust in the LORD with all thine heart; and lean not unto thine own understanding. 6 In all thy ways acknowledge him, and he shall direct thy paths. 7 Be not wise in thine own eyes: fear the LORD, and depart from evil.

When people place their trust in God, they will have victory, because the Lord has the ability to make their expectations become reality. God must be acknowledged not just sometimes, but every time, as he is the way maker. He knows the future, and he knows how to direct his children towards success. He will navigate his children away from the traps of the adversary.

22.1 Trust God for your future directions

God has a plan of a great future for his children. However, he expects that they will trust him as he leads them. When believers place their trust in God, they relieve themselves from worries, because God will do what believers are unable to do for themselves.

Psalm 32:7-10

7 Thou art my hiding place; thou shalt preserve me from trouble; thou shalt compass me about with songs of deliverance. Selah. 8 I will instruct thee and teach thee in the way which thou shalt go: I will guide thee with mine eye. 9 Be ye not as the horse, or as the mule, which have no understanding: whose mouth must be held in with bit and bridle, lest they come near unto thee. ¹⁰ *Many sorrows shall be to the wicked: but he that trusteth in the LORD, mercy shall compass him about.*

22.2 Can you trust God to protect you in difficult situations?

There will always be many challenges in life. However, those who place their trust in God can expect that he will take them through difficult situations and cause them to be victorious.

Psalm 23:2-6

² He maketh me to lie down in green pastures: he leadeth me beside the still waters. ³ He restoreth my soul: he leadeth me in the paths of righteousness for his name's sake. ⁴ Yea, though I walk through the valley of the shadow of death, I will fear no evil: for thou art with me; thy rod and thy staff they comfort me. ⁵ Thou preparest a table before me in the presence of mine enemies: thou anointest my head with oil; my cup runneth over. ⁶ Surely goodness and mercy shall follow me all the days of my life: and I will dwell in the house of the LORD for ever.

Those who trust God must know that he does not operate like humans who will run away and leave you when you are in trouble. God will stand by your side when you are going through troubles, so continue to trust him as your God.

Psalm 23:4

⁴ Yea, though I walk through the valley of the shadow of death, I will fear no evil: for thou art with me; thy rod and thy staff they comfort me.

Isaiah 43:2

² When thou passest through the waters, I will be with thee; and through the rivers, they shall not overflow thee: when thou walkest through the fire, thou shalt not be burned; neither shall the flame kindle upon thee.

The life of Job reminds us that believers can expect difficult situations, but they must never give up their trust in God. Job testified that he still had trust in God even though many things around him were failing.

Job 13:15

¹⁵ Though he slay me, yet will I trust in him: but I will maintain mine own ways before him.

23. Confidence in God

Ask God for whatever you need, according to his will, and be confident that he will bring it to pass. If you lack confidence, then you have nullified your prayer.

1 John 5:14-15

14 And this is the confidence that we have in him, that, if we ask any thing according to his will, he heareth us: 15 And if we know that he hear us, whatsoever we ask, we know that we have the petitions that we desired of him.

23.1 Have confidence in God

Animals put confidence in people, since they expect those people to provide for them and protect them. However, believers must know that while people can help them, they must place their confidence in God and not in man. Many times, people will disappoint them. People sometimes do things for others because they are expecting favors in the future.

Psalm 118:7-10

7 The LORD taketh my part with them that help me: therefore shall I see my desire upon them that hate me. 8 It is better to trust in the LORD than to put confidence in man. 9 It is better to trust in the LORD than to put confidence in princes. 10 All nations compassed me about: but in the name of the LORD will I destroy them.

Let the Lord be your confidence and not man.

Proverbs 3:26

26 For the LORD shall be thy confidence, and shall keep thy foot from being taken.

Hebrews 10:35-36

35 Cast not away therefore your confidence, which hath great recompense of reward. 36 For ye have need of patience, that, after ye have done the will of God, ye might receive the promise.

23.2 Fear God and let him build your confidence

Do not be afraid of God, but fear him. Allow him to build your confidence. While many things may look very bad on the outside, rest assured that God is with you and wants to do good for you. So, place your confidence in him.

Proverbs 14:26-28

26 In the fear of the LORD is strong confidence: and his children shall have a place of refuge. 27 The fear of the LORD is a fountain of life, to depart from the snares of death. 28 In the multitude of people is the king's honour: but in the want of people is the destruction of the prince.

23.3 Be confident that God will protect you

Those who have faith in God must be confident that God will come through for them. Their enemies may be numerous, but God will take believers through their challenging situations.

Psalm 27:3-4

3 Though an host should encamp against me, my heart shall not fear: though war should rise against me, in this will I be confident. 4 One thing have I desired of the LORD, that will I seek after; that I may dwell in the house of the LORD all the days of my life, to behold the beauty of the LORD, and to enquire in his temple.

Be willing to stay in God's presence before and after every situation. Some situations have the ability to take away your life, but God will take you through every situation and make you victorious.

24. Prayer to God

Your faith in God requires you to pray to him. Many of the things that you need God to do need your input through prayer. How do you expect God to do the impossible for you if you do not want to trust him?

While you are believing God for mountains to be moved from your life, you must pray. If you are placing your faith in God for new employment, you must pray. Hannah needed a son from God. She had faith in God, but she also spent time praying to God for him to make her faith visible (1 Samuel 1:9-21). After Hannah prayed, she left the sanctuary because she was confident that her prayer was answered.

A farmer who plants a seed is expected to water it. Similarly, believers have faith in God, and as they wait, they keep praying and praising God until they receive their victory.

24.1 King Hezekiah had faith in God, and he prayed

God informed King Hezekiah through the prophet Isaiah that he would soon die. Immediately, King Hezekiah let his faith arise. He knew of his relationship with God, and he was not going to accept death over life. He reminded God about his faithfulness unto the Lord.

King Hezekiah engaged in prayer, and instead of his life coming to a quick end, fifteen more years were added to him. Every believer who is exercising faith in God must pray. They must pray even when they do not see the evidence of that for which they are trusting the Lord.

2 Kings 20:1-11

¹In those days was Hezekiah sick unto death. And the prophet Isaiah the son of Amoz came to him, and said unto him, Thus saith the LORD, Set thine house in order; for thou shalt die, and not live. ²Then he turned his face to the wall, and prayed unto the LORD, saying, ³I beseech thee, O LORD, remember now how I have walked before thee in truth and with a perfect heart, and have done that which is good in thy sight. And Hezekiah wept sore. ⁴And it came to pass, afore Isaiah was gone out into the middle court, that the word of the LORD came to him, saying, ⁵Turn again, and tell Hezekiah the captain of my people, Thus saith the LORD, the God of David thy father, I have heard thy prayer, I have seen thy tears: behold, I will heal thee: on the third day thou shalt go up unto the house of the LORD. ⁶And I will add unto thy days fifteen years; and I will deliver thee and this city out of the hand of the king of Assyria; and I will defend this city for mine own sake, and for my servant David's sake.

⁷And Isaiah said, Take a lump of figs. And they took and laid it on the boil, and he recovered. ⁸And Hezekiah said unto Isaiah, What shall be the sign that the LORD will heal me, and that I shall go up into the house of the LORD the third day? ⁹And Isaiah said, This sign shalt thou have of the LORD, that the LORD will do the thing that he hath spoken: shall the shadow go forward ten degrees, or go back ten degrees? ¹⁰And Hezekiah answered, It is a light thing for the shadow to go down ten degrees: nay, but let the shadow return backward ten degrees. ¹¹And Isaiah the prophet cried unto the LORD: and he brought the shadow ten degrees backward, by which it had gone down in the dial of Ahaz.

Prayer demands things from a faithful God. The Lord promises to be there for his children, and he will not withhold any good thing from them, but they must pray.

Remember, Jesus said that if you have faith as a mustard seed, then the mountains shall be moved. The disciples wanted to know why certain demons were not going out, but he first reminded them that they have to have faith, and then they must pray and fast.

Matthew 17:20-21

²⁰And Jesus said unto them, Because of your unbelief: for verily I say unto you, If ye have faith as a grain of mustard seed, ye shall say unto this mountain, Remove hence to yonder place; and it shall remove; and nothing shall be impossible unto you. ²¹Howbeit this kind goeth not out but by prayer and fasting.

24.2 Whatever you are expecting from God in faith, remember to pray.

Jesus wants all believers to ask him for whatever they need. No believer must feel that their needs are too much for God to make it possible.

Jeremiah 32:27

27 Behold, I am the LORD, the God of all flesh: is there any thing too hard for me?

Remember that nothing is impossible with God. Therefore, pray for whatever you need to see, and God will make it happen for you.

Matthew 7:7-8

7 Ask, and it shall be given you; seek, and ye shall find; knock, and it shall be opened unto you: 8 For every one that asketh receiveth; and he that seeketh findeth; and to him that knocketh it shall be opened.

Reference List

Dake, Finis Jennings. *Dake Annotated Reference Bible.* Christian Art Distributors, 1992.

Easton, Matthew George. *Illustrated Bible Dictionary, and Treasury of Biblical History, Biography, Geography, Doctrine, and Literature*, 2nd ed. London: T. Nelson and Servants, 1894.

Fowler, H. W., and F. G. Fowler. *The Concise Oxford Dictionary*, 5th ed. London: Oxford University Press, 1964.

About the Author

Reverend Geary Reid has never seen God the Father, God the Son, or God the Holy Spirit, but he believes in them. He would not trade his faith in God for anything, since he has seen what God has done for him and through him. He has seen God answer his prayers for many things, because he has faith in God and did not waver in his faith.

Reverend Geary Reid is calling on believers to stop talking about faith and begin to walk in faith. Many persons are looking to believers for examples of God working through them, and Reid thinks that many believers can demonstrate their faith to the world.

As Reid studied over the years, he saw that God granted him favors. Even as he has worked for different employers, he has constantly seen the hands of God working through his life, as he has sometimes prayed for certain employees. Many times when people share their problems with him, he shares with them the God who is bigger than their problems. He reminds them to have faith in God, and many times, God proves himself to them.

Even as persons use this literature for personal devotion, Bible studies, or Bible school, they have a personal responsibility to let their faith arise. Never let your faith remain static, but cause your faith to grow. If you do not know how to grow your faith, then this literature from Reverend Reid will provide you with scriptures and practical ways of growing your faith in God.

You can join Reverend Reid in demonstrating your faith in God and not living in fear. Every mountain that stands before you can be removed if you have faith in God. Be a source of encouragement to someone today and let their faith arise.

Author Reid has used his many years of serving God to help persons to know more about faith. He provides many illustrations along with the scriptures to give persons an easy understanding of what they can do to let their faith arise. With this literature from Reverend Reid, you are now challenged to see mountains and command them to be moved, and they will obey you, as you come in the name of the Lord.

Today, you will join Reverend Reid and believe God for those things that once seemed impossible. Even when you are told that you cannot become a new champion, you will challenge the views of others, as you believe in the report of the Lord. You will pray and trust God until your needs are met. People will see great things happen through your life, and they will want to know how it happens. Just let them know that your faith has risen in God.